THE SCARLET LETTER

The woman who wears the scarlet letter on her bosom is a woman without friends, a woman who has sinned. Fingers point at her, respectable people turn their faces away from her, the priests speak hard words about her. Shame follows in her footsteps, night and day.

Because this is New England in the 1600s. The Puritans have crossed the sea to the shores of America, building their new towns, bringing their religion and their customs with them from the old country. And in the early years of Boston, in the state of Massachusetts, the church is strong – and unforgiving. Anyone who breaks the laws of the church, and of God, must be punished.

But Hester Prynne, whose husband is not her baby's father, did not sin alone. Who is the father of her child? Why does he not speak out? Why should Hester wear the scarlet letter of shame, and not her lover? Is he not guilty too?

OXFORD BOOKWORMS LIBRARY
Classics

The Scarlet Letter

Stage 4 (1400 headwords)

Series Editor: Jennifer Bassett
Founder Editor: Tricia Hedge
Activities Editors: Jennifer Bassett and Christine Lindop

NATHANIEL HAWTHORNE

The Scarlet Letter

Retold by
John Escott

Illustrated by
Thomas Sperling

OXFORD UNIVERSITY PRESS

OXFORD
UNIVERSITY PRESS

Great Clarendon Street, Oxford OX2 6DP

Oxford University Press is a department of the University of Oxford.
It furthers the University's objective of excellence in research, scholarship,
and education by publishing worldwide in

Oxford New York

Auckland Cape Town Dar es Salaam Hong Kong Karachi
Kuala Lumpur Madrid Melbourne Mexico City Nairobi
New Delhi Shanghai Taipei Toronto

With offices in

Argentina Austria Brazil Chile Czech Republic France Greece
Guatemala Hungary Italy Japan Poland Portugal Singapore
South Korea Switzerland Thailand Turkey Ukraine Vietnam

OXFORD and OXFORD ENGLISH are registered trade marks of
Oxford University Press in the UK and in certain other countries

ISBN 978 0 19 479183 0

A complete recording of this Bookworms edition of
The Scarlet Letter is available on audio CD ISBN 978 0 19 479153 3

Printed in China

Word count (main text): 15,965 words

For more information on the Oxford Bookworms Library,
visit www.oup.com/bookworms

CONTENTS

SALEM, MY HOME TOWN, is a quiet place, and not many ships call at the port here, though in the last century, before the war with Britain, the port was often busy. Now the ships go down the coast to the great sea-ports of Boston or New York, and grass grows in the streets around the old port buildings in Salem.

For a few years, when I was a young man, I worked in the port offices of Salem. Most of the time, there was very little work to do, and one day in 1849 I was looking through an old wooden box in one of the dusty, unused rooms of the building. It was full of papers about long-forgotten ships, but then something red caught my eye. I took it out and saw that it was a piece of red material, in the shape of a letter about ten centimetres long. It was the capital letter A. It was a wonderful piece of needlework, with patterns of gold thread around the letter, but the material was now worn thin with age.

It was a strange thing to find. What could it mean? Was it once part of some fashionable lady's dress long years ago? Perhaps a mark to show that the wearer was a famous person, or someone of good family or great importance?

1

I held it in my hands, wondering, and it seemed to me that the scarlet letter had some deep meaning, which I could not understand. Then I held the letter to my chest and – you must not doubt my words – experienced a strange feeling of burning heat. Suddenly the letter seemed to be not red material, but red-hot metal. I trembled, and let the letter fall upon the floor.

Then I saw that there was an old packet of papers next to its place in the box. I opened the packet carefully and began to read. There were several papers, explaining the history of the scarlet letter, and containing many details of the life and experiences of a woman called Hester Prynne. She had died long ago, sometime in the 1690s, but many people in the state of Massachusetts at that time had known her name and story.

And it is Hester Prynne's story that I tell you now. It is a story of the early years of Boston, soon after the City Fathers had built with their own hands the first wooden buildings – the houses, the churches . . . and the prison.

1

Hester Prynne's shame

On that June morning, in the middle years of the seventeenth century, the prison in Boston was still a new building. But it already looked old, and was a dark, ugly place, surrounded by rough grass. The only thing of beauty was a wild rose growing by the door, and its bright, sweet-smelling flowers seemed to smile kindly at the poor prisoners who went into that place, and at those who came out to their death.

A crowd of people waited in Prison Lane. The men all had beards, and wore sad-coloured clothes and tall grey hats. There were women, too, in the crowd, and all eyes watched the heavy wooden door of the prison. There was no mercy in the faces, and the women seemed to take a special interest in what was going to happen. They were country women, and the bright morning sun shone down on strong shoulders and wide skirts, and on round, red faces. Many of them had been born in England, and had crossed the sea twenty years before, with the first families who came to build the town of Boston in New England. They brought the customs and religion of old England with them – and also the loud voices and strong opinions of Englishwomen of those times.

'It would be better,' said one hard-faced woman of fifty, 'if we good, sensible, church-going women could judge this Hester Prynne. And would we give her the same light punishment that the magistrates give her? No!'

'People say,' said another woman, 'that Mr Dimmesdale, her priest, is deeply saddened by the shame that this woman has brought on his church.'

'The magistrates are too merciful,' said a third woman. 'They should burn the letter into her forehead with hot metal, not put it on the front of her dress!'

'She ought to die!' cried another woman. 'She has brought shame on all of us! Ah – here she comes!'

The door of the prison opened and, like a black shadow coming out into sunshine, the prison officer appeared. He put his right hand on the shoulder of a woman and pulled her forward, but she pushed him away and stepped out into the open air. There was a child in her arms – a baby of three months – which shut its eyes and turned its head away from the bright sun.

The woman's face was suddenly pink under the stares of the crowd, but she smiled proudly and looked round at her neighbours and the people of her town. On the bosom of her dress, in fine red cloth and surrounded with fantastic patterns of gold thread, was the letter A.

The young woman was tall and perfectly shaped. She had long dark hair which shone in the sunlight, and a beautiful face with deep black eyes. She walked like a lady, and those who had expected her to appear sad and ashamed were surprised how her beauty shone out through her misfortune.

*The woman smiled proudly and looked round
at the people of her town.*

But the thing that everyone stared at was the Scarlet Letter,
sewn so fantastically on to her dress.

'She is clever with her needle,' said one of the women. 'But
what a way to show it! She is meant to wear that letter as a
punishment, not as something to be proud of!'

5

The officer stepped forward and people moved back to allow the woman to walk through the crowd. It was not far from the prison to the market-place, where, at the western end, in front of Boston's earliest church, stood the scaffold. Here, criminals met their death before the eyes of the townspeople, but the scaffold platform was also used as a place of shame, where those who had done wrong in the eyes of God were made to stand and show their shameful faces to the world.

Hester Prynne accepted her punishment bravely. She walked up the wooden steps to the platform, and turned to face the stares of the crowd.

A thousand eyes fixed on her, looking at the scarlet letter on her bosom. People today might laugh at a sight like this, but in those early years of New England, religious feeling was very strong, and the shame of Hester Prynne's sin was felt deeply by young and old throughout the town.

As she stood there, feeling every eye upon her, she felt she wanted to scream and throw herself off the platform, or else go mad at once. Pictures from the past came and went inside her head: pictures of her village in Old England, of her dead parents – her father's face with his white beard, her mother's look of worried love. And her own face – a girl's face in the dark mirror where she had often stared at it. And then the face of a man old in years, a thin, white face, with the serious look of one who spends most of his time studying books. A man whose eyes seemed to see into the human soul when their owner wished it, and whose left shoulder was a little higher

than his right. Next came pictures of the tall grey houses and
great churches of the city of Amsterdam, where a new life had
begun for her with this older man.

And then, suddenly, she was back in the Boston market-
place, standing on the platform of the scaffold.

Could it be true? She held the child so close to her bosom
that it cried out. She looked down at the scarlet letter, touched
it with her finger to be sure that the child and the shame were
real. Yes – *these* things were real – everything else had
disappeared.

After a time the woman noticed two figures on the edge of
the crowd. An Indian was standing there, and by his side was
a white man, small and intelligent-looking, and wearing
clothes that showed he had been travelling in wild places. And
although he had arranged his clothes to hide it, it was clear
to Hester Prynne that one of the man's shoulders was higher
than the other.

Again, she pulled the child to her bosom so violently that
it cried out in pain. But the mother did not seem to hear it.

The man on the edge of the crowd had been looking closely
at Hester Prynne for some time before she saw him. At first,
his face had become dark and angry – but only for a moment,
then it was calm again. Soon he saw Hester staring, and knew
that she recognized him.

'Excuse me,' he said to a man near him. 'Who is this
woman, and why is she standing there in public shame?'

'You must be a stranger here, friend,' said the man, looking
at the questioner and his Indian companion, 'or you would

know about the evil Mistress Prynne. She has brought great shame on Mr Dimmesdale's church.'

'It is true,' said the stranger. 'I am new here. I have had many accidents on land and at sea, and I've been a prisoner of the wild men in the south. This Indian has helped me get free. Please tell me what brought this Hester Prynne to the scaffold.'

'She was the wife of an Englishman who lived in Amsterdam,' said the townsman. 'He decided to come to Massachusetts, and sent his wife ahead of him as he had business matters to bring to an end before he could leave. During the two years that the woman has lived here in Boston, there has been no news of Master Prynne; and his young wife, you see . . .'

'Ah! I understand,' said the stranger, with a cold smile. 'And who is the father of the child she is holding?'

'That remains a mystery,' said the other man. 'Hester Prynne refuses to speak his name.'

'Her husband should come and find the man,' said the stranger, with another smile.

'Yes, indeed he should if he is still alive,' replied the townsman. 'Our magistrates, you see, decided to be merciful. She is obviously guilty of adultery, and the usual punishment for adultery is death. But Mistress Prynne is young and good-looking, and her husband is probably at the bottom of the sea. So, in their mercy, the magistrates have ordered her to stand on the scaffold for three hours, and to wear the scarlet "A" for adultery for the rest of her life.'

'A sensible punishment,' said the stranger. 'It will warn others against this sin. However, it is wrong that the father of her child, who has also sinned, is not standing by her side on the scaffold. But he will be known! He will be known!'

The stranger thanked the townsman, whispered a few words to his Indian companion, and then they both moved away through the crowd.

During this conversation, Hester Prynne had been watching the stranger – and was glad to have the staring crowd between herself and him. It was better to stand like this, than to have to meet him alone, and she feared the moment of that meeting greatly. Lost in these thoughts, she did not at first hear the voice behind her.

'Listen to me, Hester Prynne!' the voice said again.

It was the voice of the famous John Wilson, the oldest priest in Boston, and a kind man. He stood with the other priests and officers of the town on a balcony outside the meeting-house, which was close behind the scaffold.

'I have asked my young friend' – Mr Wilson put a hand on the shoulder of the pale young priest beside him – 'to ask you once again for the name of the man who brought this terrible shame upon you. Mr Dimmesdale has been your priest, and is the best man to do it. Speak to the woman, Mr Dimmesdale. It is important to her soul, and to you, who cares about her soul. Persuade her to tell the truth!'

The young priest had large, sad brown eyes, and lips that trembled as he spoke. He seemed shy and sensitive, and his face had a fearful, half-frightened look. But when he spoke, his simple words and sweet voice went straight to people's hearts and often brought tears to their eyes.

He stepped forward on the balcony and looked down at the woman below him.

'Hester Prynne,' he said. 'If you think it will bring peace to your soul, and will bring you closer to the path to heaven, speak out the name of the man! Do not be silent because you feel sorry for him. Believe me, Hester, although he may have to step down from a high place and stand beside you on the platform of shame, it is better to do that than to hide a guilty heart through his life. Heaven has allowed you public shame, and the chance to win an open battle with the evil inside you and the sadness outside. Do you refuse to give him that same chance – which he may be too afraid to take himself?'

Hester shook her head, her face now as pale as the young priest's.

'I will not speak his name,' she said. 'My child must find a father in heaven. She will never know one on earth!'

Again she was asked, and again she refused. Then the oldest priest spoke to the crowd about all the evil in the world, and about the sin that brought the mark of the scarlet letter. For an hour or more he spoke, but Hester Prynne kept her place alone upon the platform of shame.

When the hours of punishment were over, she was taken back to the prison. And it was whispered by those who stared after her that the scarlet letter threw a terrible, ghostly light into the darkness inside the prison doors.

'I will not speak his name,' Hester said.

2

Roger Chillingworth's secret

Back inside the prison, Hester Prynne became strangely fearful and excited. The prison officer, Master Brackett, watched her carefully, afraid that she would do something violent, either to herself or to the child. By night-time, unable to quieten her, and worried about the child who screamed without stopping, Brackett decided to bring a doctor to her.

He described him to Hester as someone who had learned much about natural medicines from the Indians. But the man who followed Brackett into the prison was the man Hester had seen on the edge of the crowd earlier, the man she had watched in fear. His name, she was told, was Roger Chillingworth.

Brackett brought the man in, and stood watching in surprise as Hester became as still as death. The child, however, continued to cry.

'Please leave us alone,' Chillingworth said to the prison officer, 'and you will soon have peace in your house.'

He had entered the room calmly, carrying a small bag, and he remained calm after Brackett had left them. First he went to the child and looked carefully at her. Then he opened his bag, took out some powder, and put it into a cup of water.

'Here, woman!' he said. 'The child is yours, not mine. Give this to her.'

Hester did not move, and when she spoke, her voice was a whisper. 'Don't take your revenge on an innocent child.'

'Silly woman!' he replied, half coldly, half kindly. 'If this poor, miserable baby was my own – mine, as well as yours! – I would give her the same medicine.'

Hester still hesitated, so he took the child and gave her the medicine himself. Almost at once she became quiet, and after a moment fell peacefully asleep.

Chillingworth prepared another drink of medicine and held out the cup to Hester. 'Drink it!' he said. 'It cannot quieten your troubled soul, but it will calm you.'

She took it from him slowly, but her eyes were full of doubt about his reasons for helping her. Then she looked at her sleeping child.

'I have thought of death,' she said. 'I have wished for it, and even prayed for it, but if death is in this cup, then I ask you to think again before I drink it.'

'You need not be afraid,' he replied calmly. 'If I wanted revenge, then what more could I ask for than to let you live – and suffer, under the shadow of this shame?'

As he spoke, he put his finger on the scarlet letter, which suddenly seemed to burn red-hot on Hester's bosom.

She drank the medicine quickly, then sat down on the bed where the child was sleeping. She watched, trembling as the man she had wronged pulled up a chair and sat beside her.

'Hester,' he said, 'you've been weak, but I've been stupid.

Look at me! I'm old and ugly. I was ugly from the moment that I was born. But you? You were young and beautiful, and full of life. How could I have imagined, the day that I married you, that you would ever love me? How could a man of books and learning be so stupid?'

'I never felt or pretended any love for you,' said Hester.

'True,' he replied. 'But I hoped to make you love me.'

'I have greatly wronged you,' Hester whispered.

'We have wronged each other,' he said. 'I'm not looking for revenge, Hester. I wish you no harm. But there is a man living who has wronged us both! Who is he?'

'Do not ask me!' she cried, looking straight at him. 'You will never know his name!'

His smile was both dark and confident. 'Believe me, Hester,' he said, 'I shall know him! Although he does not wear a letter of shame on his clothes, as you do, I shall read it on his heart. I shall see it in his eyes. I shall watch him tremble, and I will feel myself tremble with him. But don't be afraid. I won't hurt him, or harm his position in the town if he is an important man here. Nor shall I inform the law. No, let him live! Let him pretend to be an honest man! Heaven will punish him for me. But I will know him!'

'You say you will not harm him,' said Hester, confused and afraid, 'but your words frighten me.'

'One thing I ask you – you, who were my wife,' he said. 'You have kept your lover's secret, now keep mine! Tell nobody that you ever called me husband. No one in this land knows me. But here, on this wild edge of the earth, I shall stay,

'Believe me,' Chillingworth said, 'I shall know him!'

because you and yours, Hester Prynne, belong to me. Love or hate, right or wrong, my home is where you are and where he is. But keep my secret!'

'Why do you want this?' said Hester, suddenly afraid of this secret agreement, although she did not know why. 'Why not say openly who you are, and send me away at once?'

15

'Perhaps because I do not want to hear what people say about a husband who loses his wife to another man,' he said. 'Let them think your husband is already dead. Pretend not to know me. Do not tell our secret to anyone, and most of all, not to your lover. Do not fail in this, Hester! Remember, his good name, his position, his life will be in my hands!'

'I will keep your secret, as I have kept his,' said Hester.

'And now, Mistress Prynne,' said the man called Roger Chillingworth, 'I will leave you alone with your child and the scarlet letter!' He smiled, slowly.

Hester stared at him, afraid of the expression in his eyes.

'Why do you smile at me?' she asked. 'Have you tied me into an agreement that will destroy my soul?'

'Not your soul,' he answered, with another smile. 'No, not yours!'

3

A fatherless child

Hester Prynne's time in prison now came to an end, but she did not move away from the town. The father of her child lived here, and here she would stay; although she kept this thought hidden guiltily in her heart. The reason she gave herself for staying was this: 'I sinned here, and I will suffer my earthly punishment here.'

There was a small cottage just outside the town, looking out across the sea towards the forest-covered hills of the west, and Hester and her child went to live in this lonely little house. They had no friends, but Hester soon found that she could earn enough money to buy food and clothes for herself and her daughter.

She was clever with a needle, and the scarlet letter which she wore on her bosom was a perfect example of her work that everyone could see. Soon, Hester's beautiful sewing, with its patterns in gold and silver thread, became the fashion with the rich and important people of the town. Her needlework was seen on the shirts of the Governor, on the fine dresses of the ladies, on the babies' little coats and hats, and on the burial-clothes of the dead. Hester had employment for as many hours as she wanted to work.

She used whatever time she had left to make clothes for the poor people of the town, although she got no thanks for it. And indeed, she found no kindness anywhere. The Puritans of that time were hard judges, and a woman who had sinned as Hester had sinned was always an outsider. Every word, every look, every cold, accusing silence reminded her of the shame and the lonely misery of her life. Even the children ran after her in the street, shouting terrible names.

She lived very simply. Her own dresses were made from dark, sad-coloured cloth, with the scarlet letter bright on the bosom. Her child's clothes were the opposite – in materials of deep, rich colours, with beautiful patterns sewn in gold thread.

Her daughter's name was Pearl. She was a pretty child, but a child of many moods – one minute bright and happy and loving, the next minute dark and angry. A child of sin, she had no right to play with the children of godly families and, like her mother, she was an outsider. In a strange way Pearl seemed to understand this, and often screamed and threw stones at the other children. Hester worried about her daughter's wildness and tried hard to correct her, but without much success. Sometimes, her only hours of peace and quietness were when Pearl was sleeping.

One day, when Pearl was about three years old, Hester went to the house of Governor Bellingham. She was taking a fine shirt she had sewn, but she also wanted to speak to the Governor in person. She had heard that many Puritans in the town wanted to take Pearl away from her. They said it would be better for the child to grow up in a more godly home than Hester Prynne's.

So it was a worried Hester who walked to the Governor's house that morning. She had dressed her daughter in a beautiful red dress, adding to the child's natural beauty, and as Pearl danced along beside her mother, it had a strange effect. The child in her red dress seemed like the scarlet letter in another shape; the scarlet letter given life and movement.

At the Governor's house the door was opened by a servant.

'Is the Governor in?' asked Hester.

'Yes,' replied the servant. 'But there are people with him at the moment. You can't see him now.'

'I'll wait,' said Hester, and stepped into the entrance hall.

The hall was wide with a high ceiling, and there were heavy chairs along one side and a long table in the centre. At the far end of the hall was a big glass door, which opened out into a garden. Hester could see rose bushes and apple trees, and Pearl immediately began to cry for a red rose.

'Shh! Be quiet, child!' said her mother. 'Look, the Governor is coming down the garden path, with three more gentlemen.'

Governor Bellingham, with his grey beard, walked in front. Behind him came John Wilson, the old priest, whose beard was as white as snow; and behind him was Arthur Dimmesdale, with Roger Chillingworth. The young priest's health had been poor for some time, and Roger Chillingworth, well known in the town for his knowledge of medicines, was now both friend and doctor to him.

19

The Governor pushed open the door – and found himself looking at Pearl, while Hester stood in the shadow of a curtain, half-hidden.

'What have we here?' said Governor Bellingham, surprised to see the little scarlet figure in front of him.

'Yes, what little bird is this?' said old Mr Wilson. 'Who are you, child?'

'My name is Pearl,' answered the little girl.

'Pearl?' replied the old priest. 'But where is your mother? Ah! I see her now.' He turned to the Governor and whispered, 'This is the child we were talking about, and look, here is the unhappy woman, Hester Prynne, her mother!'

'Is that right?' cried the Governor. 'She comes at a good time. We will discuss the matter now.' He stepped through the door into the hall, followed by his three guests. 'Hester Prynne, we have been asking many questions about you recently. Are you the right person to teach this child the ways of God, and so make sure of a place in heaven for her soul? You, a woman who has sinned! Will it not be better for her if we take her away from you, and teach her the truths of heaven and earth? What can *you* do for her, woman?'

'I can teach my little Pearl what I have learned from this!' answered Hester Prynne, putting her finger on the scarlet letter. 'Every day, it teaches me lessons that I pass on to my child. She will be a better and wiser person than I ever was.'

Bellingham turned to the old priest. 'Mr Wilson, see what this child knows,' he said.

The old priest sat down in one of the heavy chairs and tried to bring Pearl across to him, but she escaped through the open door and stood on the step outside, looking like a richly coloured bird ready to fly away.

'Pearl,' said Mr Wilson, with a serious look on his face. 'Listen to me, child. Can you tell me who made you?'

Now Pearl knew the answer very well, because Hester had told her about God many times, and had explained those things which every child should know. But Pearl put her fingers in her mouth and would not speak.

'You must answer good Mr Wilson's question,' said her mother. 'Please, Pearl! Tell him what you know.'

'My mother picked me from the wild rose bush that grows outside the prison door!' said Pearl.

Roger Chillingworth smiled and whispered something in the young priest's ear.

'This is terrible!' cried the Governor. 'The child is three years old, and she does not know who made her! I do not think, gentlemen, that we need to ask any more!'

Hester pulled Pearl towards her and held her hand. 'God gave me the child,' she cried. 'She is my happiness, my pain! You shall not take her! I will die first!'

'My poor woman,' said the old priest, kindly, 'we will find someone who will take care of the child far better than you can.'

'God gave her to me!' repeated Hester, her voice high and afraid. 'I will not let her go!' She turned to Mr Dimmesdale. 'Speak for me!' she cried. 'You were my priest, and you know me better than these men. You know what is in my heart, and

'You shall not take her! I will die first!' Hester cried.

how strongly a mother feels when she has nothing except her child and the scarlet letter!'

The young priest stepped forward, his face white and nervous, and with pain in his large dark eyes.

'There is truth in what she says,' he began. His voice was sweet and gentle, but it seemed to ring through the hall like a bell. 'God gave her the child, and is that not part of God's plan for this poor, sinful woman? With the child by her side, every day she will be reminded of her great sin, her shame; and the pain and sadness of it will always be with her. But God has given her a job to do, which will keep her soul alive and save her from further sin. She must love and care for the child, and teach it the ways of God, to know good from evil, right from wrong. And, with God's great mercy, if she brings the child to heaven, then the child also will bring its mother there! No, no, we should leave the mother and child together, and let God's gift do its work saving the mother's soul!'

'You speak, my friend, with a strange passion,' said old Roger Chillingworth, smiling at him.

'And my young friend speaks wisely,' said Mr Wilson. 'What do you think, Governor? Does he speak well for the poor woman?'

'Indeed he does,' replied Governor Bellingham. 'He argues sensibly, and so we will leave things as they are. Master Dimmesdale, you shall be responsible for making sure that the girl receives the right teaching, and that she goes to school when she is old enough to do so.'

The young priest now stood at the side of the group, his face half-hidden by the heavy window curtain. Pearl, that wild and playful little thing, moved softly towards him, took his hand, and put it gently against her cheek. Her mother watched, surprised. 'Is that my Pearl?' she thought, although she knew there was love in the child's heart. And Mr Dimmesdale looked round, put a hand on Pearl's head,

23

hesitated for a moment, then kissed her forehead. Little Pearl laughed and half-ran, half-danced down the hall.

'A strange child!' said old Roger Chillingworth. 'It is easy to see that she is her mother's daughter. But could a clever man guess, from the child's nature and from the way she behaves, the name of her father?'

'It is better to pray for an answer to that question, than to try to guess,' said Mr Wilson. 'Better still to leave it a mystery, so that every good and godly man can show a father's kindness towards the poor fatherless child.'

Hester Prynne and her daughter then left the house. As they went down the steps, a window was thrown open and a head appeared. It was Governor Bellingham's sister, Mistress Hibbins, calling down to invite Hester to a party with the Devil in the forest that night. Some people said that Mistress Hibbins was more than a little mad; others said she was truly a friend of the Devil. Mad, evil, a friend of the Devil, or all three, no one knows, but a few years later she was judged to be a witch and was killed on the scaffold.

'No, thank you!' Hester called back to her, with a smile. 'If they ever took Pearl away from me, I would go with you and sign my name in the Devil's book, even in blood! But little Pearl is still with me, and so I must stay at home and keep watch over her.'

4

A man sent by the Devil

For three years the man calling himself Roger Chillingworth had made his home in the town. Only Hester Prynne knew the secrets of his past life, which he had put behind him, but he held the lock and key to her silence and felt quite safe. His plans had changed. There were new, darker arrangements to make; new, secret things to do with his time. He had studied medicine and knew enough for other people to accept and welcome him as a doctor. Medical men were difficult to find in New England at that time.

Soon after his arrival, he became friendly with Mr Dimmesdale, and made the young man his religious guide. It was at this time, however, that the young priest's health began to fail. He grew thin and pale; his voice, though still rich and sweet, now had a sadness and tiredness about it. And sometimes, when he was alarmed by something, he would put his hand over his heart, and his eyes would fill with pain.

The young priest was greatly respected in the town; people thought he was a selfless and deeply religious man. They worried that his long hours of study and hard work for the church were damaging his health, so they were pleased when Roger Chillingworth became a friend of the young man and also offered to be his doctor. 'God has sent this man to help our priest!' they said.

But Mr Dimmesdale would not listen to his friends, and gently turned away all advice. 'I need no medicine,' he said.

But how could he say so when each week his face became paler and thinner; his voice trembled more than before; and putting his hand over his heart became a habit? Was he tired of his work? Did he wish to die?

The older priests put these questions to him, and reminded him that refusing medical help – perhaps help sent by God – was a sin. Mr Dimmesdale listened in silence, and finally promised to take advice from the doctor.

'Though if God wished it,' he said, 'I would be happy to leave behind my work, my worries and my sins and be buried in my grave.'

*   *   *

So this was how the mysterious Roger Chillingworth became the medical adviser of Mr Arthur Dimmesdale. The two men, one young and one old, began to spend much time together, walking along beside the sea or in the forest, often collecting plants to use for making medicines. Chillingworth watched and listened to his patient, asking questions carefully, digging deeper and deeper into the other man's thoughts and feelings. They spoke about public and private things; about health and religion; even about personal matters. But no secret, however much Chillingworth suspected there was one, ever came out of their discussions.

After a time, at the suggestion of Roger Chillingworth, the

friends of Mr Dimmesdale arranged for the two men to live in the same house. They thought it was the best and most sensible arrangement, at least until Mr Dimmesdale decided to marry some suitable young lady. (Although for some reason they did not understand, the young man refused to even think about marriage.) Now the good doctor could keep an even closer watch on their young friend's health.

The house was next to the town's graveyard, and Mr Dimmesdale had an apartment in the front of the building, where he could enjoy the morning sun and where there was plenty of room for his many books. In rooms on the other side of the house, Roger Chillingworth arranged his papers, and the special things needed for making medicines.

However, not all the townspeople were happy. Many people suspected that the mysterious doctor was not all he pretended to be. One old man, who had come from London more than thirty years ago, was sure that Chillingworth had lived in that city, using another name. Others spoke of the change in the man since he had come to live in the town. At first, his expression had been calm, thoughtful, the face of a man who spent his time studying. Now, there was something ugly and evil in his face. Some people even believed that Chillingworth had been sent by the Devil and was after the young priest's soul. Everyone, however, was confident that Mr Dimmesdale would be the winner of this battle.

As the months and years went by, the change in Roger Chillingworth grew greater. He had begun with the calmness of a judge, wanting only to know the truth. But as he continued, the need to know burned in him like a fever, and he dug into the priest's soul, like a man searching for gold. And poor Mr Dimmesdale, sick at heart, too afraid to call any man his friend, could not recognize an enemy either.

One day, he was in Chillingworth's room, looking out of the window at the graveyard opposite, while the older man was arranging some plants that he had collected.

'Where did you get the plants with the dark leaves?' the priest asked Chillingworth.

'From the graveyard,' answered the other man. 'I found them growing on a grave without a gravestone, or anything to tell me the dead man's name. Perhaps these black plants grew out of a heart that hid some terrible secret, one that was buried with him.'

'Perhaps the poor man wanted to tell it, but could not,' said Mr Dimmesdale. He was silent for a while, then went on, 'Tell me, doctor, is my health any better since you began to take care of this poor, weak body of mine?'

Before Chillingworth could answer, they heard a young child laughing. The sound came from the graveyard, and the priest looked down from the open window and saw Hester Prynne and little Pearl walking along the path. Pearl looked as beautiful as the day, but was behaving badly. She jumped from grave to grave, finally dancing on one of the larger graves until her mother called out to her.

'Pearl, stop it! Behave yourself!' cried Hester Prynne.

The girl stopped, but only to collect the purple flowers from a tall plant. She took a handful of them, and fastened their needle-like edges to the scarlet letter on her mother's dress. Hester did not pull them off.

Roger Chillingworth had joined Mr Dimmesdale at the window. 'That child has no respect for others,' he said, 'no idea of right or wrong. I saw her the other day throwing water at the Governor himself! What, in heaven's name, is she? A child of the devil? Has she no kindliness in her?'

'I do not know,' replied Mr Dimmesdale, quietly.

The girl probably heard their voices. She looked up, laughed, then threw one of the purple flowers at Mr Dimmesdale. And when the young priest jumped back with a little cry, she was delighted and laughed even louder.

Hester Prynne also looked up at that moment, and all four of these persons now stared at each other silently until the child laughed again, and shouted:

'Come away, mother! Come away, or that nasty old man up there will catch you! He has already caught the priest! But he won't catch little Pearl!' And she pulled her mother away, then danced off between the graves.

'There goes a woman,' said Roger Chillingworth, after a pause, 'who cannot hide her shame. It is there, for all to see. But is Hester Prynne more, or less, miserable than people who keep their sinfulness hidden?'

'I cannot answer for her,' said Mr Dimmesdale, his face pale. 'There was a look of pain in her face which it hurt me to see, but I think it must be better for sinners to be free to show their pain, as this poor woman Hester does, than to cover it all up in their heart.'

The young priest jumped back with a little cry, and Pearl laughed.

There was another pause, then the doctor said, 'You asked a little while ago for my opinion on your health.'

'I did,' said Mr Dimmesdale. 'Speak freely. Do not be afraid to tell me the truth, whether it is good news or bad.'

'Your illness is a strange one,' said Chillingworth, going back to his plants. 'I find it difficult to understand. Let me ask you, as a friend as well as your doctor, have you told me everything? Is there anything you have not told me which might help me find the true reason for your illness?'

'How can you ask?' replied the priest. 'It would be stupid to call in a doctor and then hide the injury.'

Roger Chillingworth stared hard at the other man's face. 'Yes, but the injury or evil we can see is often only half the problem,' he said. 'Sometimes it is the sickness of a man's soul that is the reason for his sick body. And then, how can a doctor help his patient to get better unless his patient tells him what is troubling his soul?'

'No, not to you!' cried Mr Dimmesdale, his eyes suddenly wild and bright. 'Only God can save a man whose sickness is a sickness of the soul! Let him do with me what he will! But who are you to involve yourself in this matter? Who are you to stand between a sufferer and his God?'

And he ran angrily from the room.

Roger Chillingworth smiled to himself. 'Nothing is lost. We shall be friends again. But look how his passion takes hold of him! He has done a wild thing before now, this godly Mr Dimmesdale, in the hot passion of his heart.'

Not long afterwards, as expected, the young priest returned and apologized. He asked his friend to continue to care for him, and the doctor agreed to do so.

* * *

A few days after this, Mr Dimmesdale falls asleep in his chair, while reading in his study. Later, Roger Chillingworth comes into the room and sees that the other man is sleeping. He steps forward, and pulls open the priest's shirt.

After a short pause, he turns away, but with what a wild look of wonder, joy, and horror!

5

A night on the scaffold

After this discovery, Roger Chillingworth's plan slowly changed. Although he appeared calm and gentle, without passion, there was inside him a deep, slow-burning cruelty, an evil wish to bring a terrible revenge on his enemy. The priest's guilty sadness was a weapon in his merciless hands. Every day he played, like a cat with a mouse, with the fear and the shame lying hidden in the young man's soul.

But on the outside he was still a friend, kindly and smiling. Arthur Dimmesdale could feel something evil watching him, but he did not know what it was. He looked with doubt and fear – at times even with hate – at the figure of the old doctor; then he would punish himself for these unkind thoughts, blaming them on the guilt and shame eating away at his heart.

And all this black trouble in his soul had made him more famous and popular as a priest than ever. To the people in his church, he seemed very close to God, a man full of gentleness and understanding of the pain and suffering of others.

More than once, Mr Dimmesdale prepared himself to speak to his people about the black secret of his soul. More than once he stood in front of them in church, took a deep breath, and told them . . . what? He told them he was the worst of sinners, hateful, dishonest, unclean, an evil thing in the sight of God. But did they understand? No! They listened, and then told each other how lucky they were to have a man like this for their priest. Only a strong and godly man, they said, could speak so openly about his weaknesses.

Arthur Dimmesdale could find no peace in his heart. He could not sleep at night, but would sit staring at his face in a mirror, hour after hour. Often, as he looked, his own face would be replaced by the accusing faces of others – dead friends from long ago, his white-bearded father, his mother. And worst of all, Hester Prynne, walking with little Pearl and pointing her finger first at the scarlet letter on her bosom, and then at the priest's own chest.

One sleepless summer night, seven years from the time when Hester stood in public shame on the scaffold, the priest sat up suddenly in his chair. An idea had come to him.

'There might be a moment's peace in it,' he said to himself, and softly went down the stairs and out into the night.

He walked silently through the dark streets to the place of Hester Prynne's first hours of public shame – the scaffold. The priest went up the steps to the platform.

It was midnight, and the town was asleep. Clouds covered the sky, and Mr Dimmesdale could stand there until morning without fear of discovery. Why, then, was he here? What had made him come? Guilt? Shame? He did not know. But a feeling of great horror went through his whole body, and he cried out a terrible scream, which echoed through the

33

night, from one house to another and to the hills beyond the town.

'It is done!' whispered the priest, covering his face with his hands. 'The whole town will wake up and find me here.'

But the people of the town did not wake up, or if they did, they imagined the cry was something which came from their dreams. When he heard no sounds of feet hurrying towards him, the young priest uncovered his eyes and looked around. At a window in Governor Bellingham's house, which was not far away, he saw the Governor himself, in his white nightshirt, with a light in his hand.

'He looks like a ghost,' thought Mr Dimmesdale. And after a moment, the light disappeared from the window.

The priest became calmer. Then he noticed another light, coming towards him along the street. As it came nearer, he saw that the person carrying it was the old priest, Mr Wilson.

'He has been praying at the bedside of some dying man,' thought Mr Dimmesdale.

And so he had. The old priest was now on his way home from the death-bed of Mr Winthrop, who had just died.

As Mr Wilson passed by the scaffold, Mr Dimmesdale found it difficult not to speak . . .

'Good evening to you, Father! Please come up and spend a pleasant hour with me!'

Good heavens! Had Mr Dimmesdale actually spoken? For one moment he believed that these words had passed his lips, but he had only imagined them. Mr Wilson walked on, looking ahead, not once turning towards the platform.

'I shall be too cold to move soon,' Mr Dimmesdale thought. 'I won't even be able to walk down the steps.' Crazy pictures passed before his eyes. 'Someone will find me here in the early morning, and will run around knocking on doors. Everyone will hurry out in their night-clothes – Governor Bellingham, with his buttons undone; his sister, mad Mistress Hibbins, staring with her wild eyes; and good Father Wilson too, tired after spending half the night at a death-bed. Yes, everyone in the world will come running! And who will they see? They will see their priest, half-frozen to death, covered with shame, and standing where Hester Prynne once stood!'

Now he began to laugh, loudly and wildly, unable to stop himself. Then he heard an answering laugh – a child's laugh – and his heart jumped. It was little Pearl.

'Pearl!' he cried. 'Little Pearl!' Then more softly, 'Hester! Hester Prynne, are you there?'

'Yes, it is me,' Hester Prynne replied. She sounded surprised. 'It is me, and my little Pearl.'

'Where have you come from, Hester?' he asked.

'From Mr Winthrop's death-bed,' she said. 'I've measured him for his burial-clothes, and I am now going home.'

'Come up here, Hester, you and little Pearl,' said the priest. 'You have both been here before, but I was not with you. Come up now, and all three of us shall stand together.'

Hester silently climbed up the steps and stood on the platform, holding Pearl's hand. The priest found and held the child's other hand, and immediately felt a warm, strong feeling in his heart, filling it with new life.

Pearl looked up at the priest. 'Will you stand here with mother and me tomorrow, Mr Dimmesdale?' she whispered.

'No, my little Pearl,' answered the priest. The moment of passionate feeling had passed. Already, he was trembling, and all his fear of public shame had returned. 'I shall stand with you and your mother one day, but not tomorrow.'

'When?' Pearl asked. 'What day?' She tried to pull her hand away from the priest's.

'The great judgement day,' he whispered. 'Then, and there, your mother and I must stand together. But not before then; not in the daylight of this world.'

Before he had finished speaking, a light appeared, far and wide in the night sky. It was almost certainly caused by a meteor, and it lit up the whole street like day. And there stood the priest, with his hand over his heart; and Hester Prynne, with the scarlet letter on her bosom; and little Pearl standing between these two, looking up at the priest with a playful smile. She pointed across the street, but he put both his hands across his chest and looked up at the sky.

However, he knew that little Pearl was pointing her finger at a man standing near the scaffold – Roger Chillingworth. Did the priest see him too? Or, in the strange unearthly light, did he see only the evil smile, the hate behind the eyes, and believe that he was seeing the Devil himself?

The meteor disappeared as suddenly as it had appeared. Mr Dimmesdale, now trembling with terror, said, 'Who is that man, Hester? Do you know him? I hate him, Hester!'

She remembered her promise, and was silent.

The priest knew that little Pearl was pointing her finger at Roger Chillingworth.

'Who is he? Who is he?' cried Mr Dimmesdale. 'Can you do nothing for me? I have a horror of the man!'

'I can tell you who he is,' said little Pearl.

'Quickly, then, child,' said the priest. 'Whisper to me!'

But the child whispered meaningless words into the priest's ear, and laughed.

'Why are you playing games with me?' said the priest.

'You would not promise to hold my hand, and my mother's hand, here tomorrow,' replied the child.

The doctor was now by the platform. 'Mr Dimmesdale!' he said. 'Have you been walking in your sleep? Come, my dear friend, let me take you home.'

'How did you know I was here?' asked the priest, fearfully.

'I did not know,' said Chillingworth. 'I have been with Mr Winthrop, doing what little I could for a dying man. Now I am on my way home. Come with me, please, or you will not be well enough to do your work tomorrow. You should not study so hard, good sir!'

'I will go home with you,' said Mr Dimmesdale, defeated. And, like someone waking up from an ugly dream, he followed the doctor back to their house.

6

Hester meets the enemy

That meeting with Mr Dimmesdale on the scaffold worried Hester Prynne greatly. She saw the young priest's weakness and his misery, and how close he was to madness; she heard the terror in his voice as he asked her for help. And she decided he had a right to all the help she could give him.

Her position in the town was now rather different. In the seven years since Pearl was born, Hester had worn the scarlet letter patiently and had led a hard-working and blameless life. People no longer hated her; some even respected her.

'She is always ready to give what she can to the poor,' they said, 'although she gets little thanks for the food she takes to them, or the clothes she makes for them.'

And whenever a house was darkened by trouble, Hester was there with warm and kindly words, and the offer of help. But when sunshine came again, she left without looking back or waiting for the grateful thanks of those who had been troubled. And afterwards, when she saw them in the street, she did not lift her head to speak to them but put her finger on her scarlet letter of shame, and passed by.

Beneath her calmness, however, there had often been great loneliness and suffering. These had made her strong and she now felt able to face the man who had once been her husband. It was clear to Hester that this man was the priest's secret enemy, playing the part of a friend and helper, and slowly but surely driving the priest into madness.

In short, she decided to talk to Roger Chillingworth, and to do what she could to stop his cruel and evil revenge.

She did not have long to wait. One afternoon, while walking with Pearl along the beach, she saw the old doctor with a basket in one hand and a stick in the other. He was collecting plants.

'Go down to the water and play while I talk to this gentleman,' Hester told her daughter.

The child flew away like a bird, her small white feet making patterns in the wet sand at the edge of the sea. Her mother walked up to Roger Chillingworth.

'I would like to speak to you,' she said.

'Ah! Mistress Hester!' he answered. 'I hear news of your good work from everyone I speak to. Only yesterday a magistrate whispered to me that the officers of the town were discussing whether the scarlet letter could now be taken off your bosom. "You should do it at once," I told him.'

'It is not for some magistrate to take off this letter,' Hester replied calmly. 'When – if ever – I earn the right to be rid of it, it will fall off without anyone's help.'

'Wear it, then, if you want to,' said Chillingworth. 'It is a fine piece of needlework and looks well on your bosom.'

While they spoke, Hester had been watching him closely and was full of wonder at the change she saw in him. He was no longer the calm, intelligent man she remembered; now there was a cruel, searching look in his eyes, and a cold half-smile came and went on his face. Seven years of getting enjoyment from a cruel revenge had left the Devil's mark on him. 'His soul seems to be on fire!' Hester thought.

'I want to speak to you about Mr Dimmesdale,' she said.

'And what about him?' cried Roger Chillingworth. 'Speak freely, and I will answer.'

'When we last spoke together, seven years ago,' Hester said, 'you made me promise not to tell anyone that we once lived as husband and wife. I agreed to be silent because, as you said then, his position and his life were in your hands. But I see now that I was wrong to keep silent. Since that day, you have been beside him, sleeping and waking. You search his thoughts and his heart, and each day you cause him to die a living death! And it is I who have allowed this to happen!'

'What else can you do?' asked Chillingworth. 'A word from me, and this man would be thrown from his church into a prison – and from there, to the scaffold!'

'Perhaps that would be better!' said Hester. 'Haven't you had your revenge? Hasn't he suffered enough for his sins?'

'No!' answered the doctor. 'Do you remember me, Hester, as I was nine years ago? You thought I was cold, perhaps, but was I not kind and true, and a good friend to others?'

'Yes,' said Hester. 'All that, and more.'

'And what am I now?' he asked, and his face showed the evil that was in him. 'A devil! And who made me this?'

41

'It was me,' said Hester, trembling. 'Me, as much as he. So why didn't you punish me?'

'You had the scarlet letter,' he said. 'That was enough revenge for me.' He put his finger on it with a smile. 'Now, what do you want to say about this man?'

'I must tell him the truth about you,' said Hester. 'He must know who you are, and why you are doing this to him. What the result will be, I do not know. Do what you want with him.

'You had the scarlet letter,' said Chillingworth.
'That was enough revenge for me.'

But there is no good for him, no good for me, no good for you, no good for little Pearl. There is no path to guide any of us out of this misery.'

Roger Chillingworth stared at the tall, proud woman in front of him, and heard the pain in her voice. Did he then remember the love he had once felt for her?

'I am sorry for you,' he said. 'You were a good person, and you needed a better love than mine.'

'And I am sorry for you,' said Hester, 'and for the hate that has changed a wise and merciful man into a devil! Try to be human again! Forgive, and leave judgement to God!'

'That is not possible,' replied the old man. 'You planted the evil, and now its black flowers are growing. We cannot change the way things are.'

He turned and walked away, and a dark shadow seemed to follow him along the ground.

Hester stared after him. 'I hate the man!' she whispered to herself. 'How I wish I had never married him!' She turned to look for her child. 'Pearl! Little Pearl! Where are you?'

The child had been busy while her mother had been talking. First she had played at the edge of the water, then she had made little boats out of pieces of wood. Then, seeing some birds feeding on the beach, she had picked up some stones and thrown them until one little grey bird had flown away with a broken wing. For her last game, Pearl collected some grass and used it to make a letter A on her chest.

'Will Mother ask me what it means?' she wondered.

Then she heard her mother calling and, moving as lightly

43

as one of the little sea-birds, she appeared beside Hester and pointed her finger towards the letter A on her bosom.

'My little Pearl,' said Hester, after a moment's silence, 'the green letter means nothing on your childish bosom. But do you know why your mother wears it?'

'Oh, yes!' said Pearl, smiling. 'It is for the same reason that the priest puts his hand over his heart!'

'And what reason is that?' asked Hester.

'I don't know,' replied Pearl. 'Mother, what does this scarlet letter mean? Why do you wear it on your bosom? And why does the priest keep his hand over his heart?'

Hester stared down into her daughter's black eyes. What should she say? The truth? No! If that was the price of the child's understanding, she could not pay it.

'Silly Pearl!' she said. 'There are many things in this world that a child must not ask about. What do I know about the priest's heart? And as for the scarlet letter, I wear it for its gold thread.'

It was the first time that Hester had lied about the letter, and the child did not stop asking the same questions. Two or three times on the way home, several times at supper, and again the next morning, Pearl asked, 'Mother, Mother, what does the scarlet letter mean?' and 'Why does the priest keep his hand over his heart?'

'Stop it!' Hester said, in a sharper voice than she had ever used before. 'Stop it, or I'll shut you in the dark cupboard!'

7

A walk in the forest

For several days, Hester Prynne waited for a chance to speak privately with Mr Dimmesdale. She would not go to his house because she was afraid of meeting Roger Chillingworth. Then she heard that the priest had gone to visit a family a little distance away and would be returning the next afternoon, through the forest. 'Come, Pearl,' she said the next day. 'We are going for a walk in the forest.'

The trees were tall and close together, and the path through them was dark and narrow under a grey sky.

'Mother,' said little Pearl, 'the sunshine does not love you. It runs away and hides itself because it is afraid of something on your bosom. But it will not run away from me, because I do not wear anything on my bosom yet.'

'And never will, my child, I hope,' said Hester. 'Now, run away and catch the sunshine.'

Pearl ran off, and Hester smiled when she saw that her child had found a circle of sunshine between the trees. But when Hester came near to it, Pearl said, 'It will go now.'

Hester smiled. 'Look, I can put out my hand and hold some of it.' But when she put her hand into the circle, the sunshine disappeared.

They walked on. Then Hester saw someone coming and said, 'Go and play by the river, child, and leave me to speak to the gentleman who is coming.'

'Who is it?' said Pearl.

'Can't you see?' said Hester. 'It is the priest.'

'And he has his hand over his heart!' said Pearl.

'Go now, child, but not too far beyond the river.'

When Pearl had gone, Hester waited under the trees. The priest walked slowly, but he had almost gone by before Hester could find her voice.

'Arthur Dimmesdale!' she said, quietly at first, then louder. 'Arthur Dimmesdale!'

'Who speaks?' he said, turning quickly. He saw a shadow under the trees, and then he saw the scarlet letter. 'Hester! Hester Prynne! Is it you?'

'It is me,' she answered.

He touched her hand, and his touch was as cold as death. They moved back into the shadows of the trees and sat down on a fallen branch. At first they spoke of the weather, the grey sky, the coming storm, but then the priest looked into Hester's eyes.

'Have you found peace?' he said.

She smiled sadly, and looked down at her bosom. 'Have you?' she asked.

'None! Nothing but misery!' he answered. 'But what else could I expect? You wear your scarlet letter openly, on your bosom, Hester. Mine burns in secret! It is good, after these seven years, to talk to someone who knows the truth. If I had one friend – or even an enemy – whom I could talk to openly each day, then perhaps it would save me. But now it is all lies, all emptiness, all death!'

Hester Prynne looked into his face. 'You have the friend that you wish for; someone to cry with you over your sin. You have me, your partner in sin.' She hesitated, then went on, 'And you have an enemy, and you live with him in the same house.'

The priest jumped up and put his hand over his heart. 'What are you saying? An enemy!' he cried. 'In the same house? What do you mean?'

'Oh, Arthur!' she cried. 'Forgive me! In all things except one, I have been true to you. But I agreed to keep a secret. I did it to save your position, Arthur, your work as a priest, here in the town. But I cannot keep the secret any more. I must tell you. The doctor – the old man they call Roger Chillingworth – he was my husband!'

The priest stared at her for a moment – a black, violent look on his face. Then he dropped down on to his knees and buried his face in his hands.

'Why didn't I guess it?' he said quietly. 'Or perhaps I did! The horror in my heart when I first saw him, and when I see him now . . . Why didn't I understand? Oh, Hester Prynne, you don't know the horror and shame this news brings me! He has been secretly laughing at my sick and guilty heart. Woman, I cannot forgive you for this!'

'You will forgive me!' cried Hester. 'Let God punish me! You shall forgive me!'

47

'Woman, I cannot forgive you for this!' said the priest.

She fell to her knees beside him, put her arms around him, and pulled his head against her bosom, not caring that his face rested on the scarlet letter. She could not allow him to hate her. 'For seven long years, all the world has blamed and hated me,' she thought. 'But I shall die if this weak, sinful, unhappy man hates me too.'

'Will you forgive me, Arthur?' she repeated, again and again. 'Don't hate me! Forgive me, please!'

'I forgive you, Hester,' the priest replied at last. His voice was sad, but not angry. 'May God forgive us both! We are not the worst sinners in the world. That old man's revenge has been blacker than our sin, Hester!'

'Yes!' she whispered. 'We loved one another, we told each other. Have you forgotten it?'

'Shh! Hester,' said Arthur Dimmesdale, getting up from the ground. 'No, I have not forgotten!'

They sat down on the tree branch, holding each other's hands. Around them, the trees were dark, and the branches moved noisily in the wind.

'What will Roger Chillingworth do now?' asked the priest. 'Will he continue to keep our secret?'

'He has a secret nature, and I think he will,' said Hester. 'But he will doubtless find other ways to take his revenge.'

'And me! How can I live in the same house, breathing the same air with this deadly enemy?' said Mr Dimmesdale, his hand over his heart again. 'Think for me, Hester! You are strong! Tell me what to do!'

'You must not stay with this evil man,' said Hester.

'But where can I go? I cannot hide from God,' he said.

'God will show mercy,' replied Hester, 'if you are strong enough to take advantage of it.'

'Be strong for me!' he answered. 'Advise me what to do.'

'Is the world so small, then?' said Hester, looking into his eyes. 'Is there nothing beyond this little town? Walk a few miles from here, and the yellow leaves will show no sign of a white man's feet. There you can be free! A short journey will take you from a world where you have been miserable, to one where you may still be happy! Then there is the sea. It brought you here, and if you choose, it can take you back again. Perhaps to London, or to Germany, or France, or pleasant Italy. You'll be beyond Roger Chillingworth there.'

'I can't do it!' answered the priest. 'I cannot walk away and leave my work. Although my own soul is lost, I must do what I can for the other human souls in my care.'

'After seven years of misery, you must leave it all behind you!' said Hester, with passion in her voice. 'Begin again. There is happiness to be enjoyed, there is good to be done. Change this false life for a true one! Teach, write! Work among the Indians! Do anything, except lie down and die! Why wait another day in this place? Go now!'

'Oh, Hester!' cried Arthur Dimmesdale. 'I am not strong enough, nor brave enough, to go out into the wide, strange, difficult world alone.'

Sadly, hopelessly, he repeated the word.

'Alone, Hester!'

'You shall not go alone,' she answered, her voice a deep whisper.

8
Hope for the future

Arthur Dimmesdale stared at Hester, with hope, joy and fear in his face. In his heart, he had thought of this too, but only Hester had been brave enough to put it into words. Suddenly, he knew that he wanted this better life that she described; and knew also that he could not live without her. 'God, will you forgive me?' he thought.

'You will go,' said Hester, calmly, as he looked at her.

And so it was decided. At once, a strange feeling of happiness came over him; something which he had thought was dead in him.

'Oh, Hester, God has been merciful!' he cried. 'This is already a better life. Why did we not find it sooner?'

'Let us not look back,' she answered. 'The past is gone! Look!' And she pulled the scarlet letter from her bosom and threw it in among the trees.

She breathed deeply. 'I did not realize how heavy it was until I was free of it!' she thought. Next, she pulled off her hat, and her hair fell down upon her shoulders, dark and rich, softening her face as it did so. She smiled, and her eyes were bright. Suddenly, she was young and beautiful again, and filled with happiness!

Another thought came into her head and she looked at him and smiled. 'You must learn to know Pearl!' she said. 'Our little Pearl. You have seen her – yes, I know you have – but you will see her now with fresh eyes. She is strange, and difficult to understand, but you will love her, and advise me what to do with her.'

'Do you think the child will be glad to know me?' asked the priest, looking worried. 'Children do not usually like me, and I have even been afraid of little Pearl.'

'That is sad,' said Hester. 'But she will love you. Let me call her. Pearl! Pearl!'

The child heard her mother's voice. She had been picking flowers and had put them in her hair and her clothes, but now she came slowly through the trees, to the other side of the little river. Very slowly – because she saw the priest.

They watched her coming.

'How strangely beautiful she looks with those flowers in her hair,' said Hester. 'She is a wonderful child! But I know whose forehead she has!'

'It is a terrible thing to say, but I have often been afraid that others would see a likeness to me in her face, and guess,' said Mr Dimmesdale. 'But she looks much more like you.'

'Do not let her see anything strange,' said Hester. 'Do not be too excited, or too loving. She will not understand. But she will love you in time.'

Pearl had stopped on the other side of the water and was looking at Hester and the priest.

'Come, dear child!' called Hester. 'How slow you are! Here

is a friend of mine, who will soon be a friend of yours also. You will have twice as much love, from today. Now, hurry up!'

Pearl did not move. She looked first at her mother, with wild bright eyes, then at the priest. Then she put out a hand and pointed at her mother's bosom.

'You strange child!' said Hester. 'Why don't you come to me? Hurry, or I shall be angry with you.'

The child began to scream, still pointing her finger accusingly at her mother's bosom.

'I know what is wrong,' Hester whispered to the priest. 'She is missing something that she has always seen me wearing.'

'If you can quieten her, please do!' said Mr Dimmesdale.

Hester, her face pale again, turned to the child. 'Pearl,' she said sadly, 'look down beside your feet. There! The other side of the river.'

The child looked round and saw the scarlet letter lying at the edge of the water.

'Bring it to me,' said Hester.

'Come and fetch it!' answered Pearl.

'The child is right about the letter, of course,' Hester said to the priest. 'I must wear it for a few more days, until we have left. The forest cannot hide it, but the sea will drown it.'

She stepped forward and, picking up the scarlet letter, fastened it to her bosom again. Next, she put up her hair again, underneath her hat. A grey shadow seemed to fall across her as she did these things. She put out a hand to Pearl.

'Do you recognize your mother now, child?' she said. 'Will you come to me now?'

53

*The child began to scream, pointing her finger
at her mother's bosom.*

'Yes, now I will,' answered the child, and jumped across the water. 'Now you are my mother, and I am your little Pearl!' Gently, she pulled down her mother's head and kissed her. Then she kissed the scarlet letter, too.

'That was not kind!' said Hester. 'You show me a little love, but then you make a joke of it!'

'Why is the priest sitting over there?' asked Pearl.

'He is waiting to welcome you,' said Hester. 'He loves you, my little Pearl, and he loves your mother, too. Come! Will you not love him?'

'Does he love us?' said Pearl, looking closely at her mother's face. 'Will he go back with us, hand in hand, the three of us together, into the town?'

'Not now, dear child,' said Hester. 'But soon he will walk hand in hand with us. We will have a home of our own, and you will sit on his knee and he will teach you many things, and love you dearly. You will love him – won't you?'

'And will he always keep his hand over his heart?' asked Pearl.

'Silly child! What kind of question is that?' said Hester. 'Come, and be nice to him.'

But Pearl made an ugly face and tried to pull away from her mother. And when Mr Dimmesdale kissed her gently on the forehead, she ran down to the river and washed her face, again and again, until the unwelcome kiss was washed away. Then she watched silently as her mother and the priest talked quietly, making arrangements for their new life together.

The plan was soon made. It was decided between them that

the Old World, with its crowds and cities, would offer them a better chance of living quietly and privately. And luckily, Hester knew of a ship which had recently arrived from Spain and would soon leave again to sail to Bristol, in England.

'I know the captain,' she said, 'and I can secretly arrange for you, me and little Pearl to sail with him to England.'

'When does the ship leave?' asked Mr Dimmesdale.

'Probably four days from today,' replied Hester.

*   *   *

As he hurried back to the town, leaving Hester and Pearl to return to their cottage, Mr Dimmesdale thought about the plan. 'Four days' time is just right. Three days from today I have to give my Election Sermon, and it will be a most suitable way to end my time here as a priest. At least they will not be able to say that I left without doing my job until the very end!'

He became more and more excited as he made his way back into the town. In this new, happier mood, everything looked and seemed different, even the people he met or passed in the street. He wanted to say to them, 'I am not the man you think I am! I left him behind in the forest!'

Then he passed Mistress Hibbins, the Governor's sister, who, unusually, stopped to speak to him.

'So, Mr Dimmesdale,' she said, 'you have been walking in the forest! You must tell me next time you plan to go. I will come with you, and we can meet our Master.' And she passed on by, giving the priest a secret little smile.

'Why does she talk to me like this?' he thought nervously. 'Does she see the black mark of the Devil in my soul?'

He was glad to reach his house, and hurried upstairs to his study. Here were his books, the window, the fireplace. Here, he had written and studied and prayed. There on the table, with his pen beside it, was the half-finished Election Sermon, which he had left behind two days ago. Now, he saw all these things differently, through the eyes of another man – a wiser man, who had returned out of the forest.

At that moment, there was a knock at his door. 'Come in!' cried Mr Dimmesdale, wondering if a devil would enter. Then old Roger Chillingworth came in, and the priest stood, unable to speak, with his hand over his heart.

'Welcome home, sir,' said the doctor, smiling. 'How was your journey through the forest? You look pale! I think you will need my help if you are going to be able to give your Election Sermon in a day or two. Don't you think so?'

'No – not at all,' replied Mr Dimmesdale. 'The long walk in the fresh air has been good for me, after spending so much time in my study. Thank you, but I do not think I need any more of your medicine, my kind doctor.'

Did Roger Chillingworth know, the priest wondered, that he had met and talked with Hester Prynne? Did he know that in the priest's eyes he was now a hated enemy? Perhaps the friendly words from the doctor to his patient now had double meanings.

'But, my dear sir, we must do whatever we can to make you strong and well,' said Chillingworth. 'The people expect great things from you, and are afraid that in another year you may be gone.'

'Yes, gone to another world,' replied the priest, sadly. 'And may God make it a better one, because I don't expect to be with my people for another year. But, thank you, sir, I do not need your medicine at the moment.'

'I am glad to hear it,' said Chillingworth.

'I thank you from my heart, most watchful friend,' said the priest. 'I can only repay your kindness with my prayers.'

'A good man's prayers are like gold!' answered Roger Chillingworth, as he went out of the room.

After he had gone, Mr Dimmesdale threw away his half-written Election Sermon and sat down to begin it again. All through that night he wrote – and the words seemed to come from God.

'A good man's prayers are like gold!' said Roger Chillingworth.

9

Escape

On the morning of Election Day, when the townspeople came together to meet their newly elected Governor, Hester Prynne came into the market-place in her usual dress of grey cloth, with the scarlet letter on her bosom. The quiet, sad look on her face hid the excitement deep inside her. Who in the crowd could guess her thoughts that day?

Look for the last time at the scarlet letter and its wearer! In a little while I will be beyond your reach! I will be free, and the scarlet letter of shame, which has burned on my bosom for seven long years, will lie for ever at the bottom of the sea!

Little Pearl, sensitive to her mother's excitement without knowing the reason for it, was dancing along at Hester's side, singing or giving happy little shouts.

'Why are the people not working today, Mother?' she asked, when she saw the crowd in the market-place. 'And look how many strangers there are here today – Indians and sailors among them. What is everyone waiting for?'

'They are waiting to see the new Governor go past,' answered Hester. 'And the magistrates and the priests, and all the great and good people, with the soldiers marching in front of them to the music.'

'Will Mr Dimmesdale be there?' asked Pearl. 'Will he hold out both his hands to me, as he did that day in the forest?'

'He will be there, child,' said Hester. 'But he will not speak to you today, and you must not speak to him.'

'What a strange, sad man he is,' said the child. 'He held your hand and mine at night on the scaffold, and again in the forest. But here on this sunny day, among all the people, he does not know us, and we must not speak to him. What a strange, sad man, with his hand always over his heart.'

'Be quiet, Pearl!' said Hester. 'You don't understand these things. Don't think about the priest. Look around, and see how happy everyone is today, on this holiday.'

And it was true. Most people were smiling, and there was a lot of talk and laughter. The sailors from the Spanish ship, with their sun-burnt faces and long beards, were noisier than most. They shouted and laughed, and drank wine from bottles. Sailors in those days obeyed only the laws of the sea, and were allowed to do much as they liked on land. Even the Puritans smiled at their noisy ways.

So it was no surprise to anyone to see a respectable man like old Roger Chillingworth come into the market-place, speaking with the captain of the ship.

Moments later, when the two men went their separate ways, the captain walked across to Hester Prynne. As usual, people avoided standing near her, which meant that she and the captain could talk privately.

'So, mistress,' said the captain, 'another one to join you! And with *two* doctors – our own ship's doctor and this other doctor – we need not fear ship-fever on this voyage!'

'What do you mean?' said Hester, alarmed. 'You have another passenger?'

'Didn't you know that this doctor – Chillingworth, he calls himself – has decided to travel with you?' said the captain. 'Oh, but you must know! He told me he's a good friend of the gentleman you spoke about.'

'They – they know each other well,' agreed Hester, trying desperately to look calm. 'They live in the same house.'

No more words were spoken between them, but at that moment she saw old Roger Chillingworth, standing in a far corner of the market-place. He was smiling at her – a smile which, even across the wide and busy square, carried secret and fearful meaning.

Before she could think clearly again, there was the sound of music, and a moment later she saw the band coming, followed by soldiers. Little Pearl laughed and jumped up and down excitedly. Next came the magistrates, and then the priests. Mr Dimmesdale was among them, but although his feet marched with the music, it is doubtful whether he actually heard it, as he seemed to be deep in thought.

Hester watched him, and her heart was heavy. Was this the same man who had sat with her in the forest, holding her hand? He looked so different now, walking proudly, with his head held high, and without a single look at her.

'It was a dream,' she thought. 'There can be no real love between us. How can there be? A man in his position.'

Pearl noticed the sadness which had suddenly come over

Chillingworth's smile carried secret and fearful meaning.

her mother, and became worried and uncomfortable. When the priests had gone by, she looked into her mother's face and said, 'Is that the same priest who kissed me in the forest?'

'Be quiet, little Pearl!' whispered her mother. 'We must not talk in the market-place about the things that happen to us in the forest!'

Then she heard her name spoken, and turned to see Mistress Hibbins behind her.

'Now, who would believe it?' the old lady whispered to Hester. 'Look at our priest, Mr Dimmesdale! He looks so *godly* today! And only a little while since he went from his study to walk in the forest! Ah! And we know what *that* means, Hester Prynne! Can you be sure, Hester, that he is the same man that you met among the trees?'

'Mistress Hibbins, I don't know what you are talking about,' said Hester. Was the old woman as mad as she seemed? Did she really dance in the forest with the Evil One, the Devil himself?

'Come, come, Hester! The Dark One knows those who have signed their names in his book!' And laughing crazily, Mistress Hibbins walked on.

By this time, the first prayers had been said in the church meeting-house, and Hester could hear Mr Dimmesdale beginning his sermon. She stood close to the scaffold platform where she could hear most of his words.

His voice was strong and clear and sweet. Sometimes he spoke quietly, and at other times with great passion. But Hester, who knew the guilt and misery in his heart, could hear in his voice a cry of pain. A cry from the very soul of the man! She listened, unable to move from the scaffold, that place of public shame which she knew so well.

Little Pearl, meanwhile, had moved away and was playing and dancing about in the market-place. Whenever she saw something which interested her, she ran across to it. She ran to stare at a group of Indians, then ran into the centre of a group of sailors, who laughed and tried to join in her game, but she would not let them.

The captain tried to kiss her, but she danced away. Then he called to her.

'Your mother is the woman with the scarlet letter, isn't she?' he said. 'Will you give her a message? Tell her that I spoke with the old doctor, and he will bring the other gentleman to the ship with him. She need only take herself and you. Will you tell her that?'

Pearl ran through the crowd to her mother, and repeated the captain's words. Hester listened with a growing misery. The plan for herself and the priest now seemed hopeless.

And even as she suffered this great disappointment, a crowd was coming together around Hester, mostly people from the countryside who had heard about but not seen 'the woman with the scarlet letter' and wanted to stare at her. The Indians, too, came to look.

And while Hester stood in the centre of that circle of shame, Mr Arthur Dimmesdale stood in the church and received the love and respect of all who listened to him.

When he finished his sermon, there was silence inside the meeting-house. A minute later, the crowd began to leave the church, all talking at once. How beautifully their good Mr Dimmesdale had spoken, they said! What a wise and godly man he was!

There was a sadness too, not in the words themselves but in the way he spoke them. A sadness of someone who is about to die. Yes, their priest, whom they loved, and who loved them, had the sound of a man who would not be in this world for much longer.

And Mr Dimmesdale? It was his proudest moment.

Now the band began to play again, and the soldiers got ready to lead everyone to the town hall. The people stepped back to make room for the Governor, the magistrates, the officers of the town, and the priests. They shouted and waved, but the noise began to die away as the crowd saw their young priest, Mr Dimmesdale.

How weak and pale he looked, suddenly! Where was the proud man who had marched to the church earlier; the man who had spoken with such passion in the meeting-house? His face was the face of a man already half-dead.

One of the other priests, old Mr Wilson, stepped forward to offer his help, but Mr Dimmesdale waved him away. They were near the scaffold now, and there stood Hester Prynne, holding little Pearl's hand. And there was the scarlet letter on her bosom. Arthur Dimmesdale stopped, unable to go on. And then he turned to the scaffold and held out his arms.

'Hester,' he said, 'come here! Come, my little Pearl!'

His face had the look of a man, both sad and joyful, who has finally won a battle inside himself.

The child ran to him and threw her arms around his knees. Hester Prynne, moving slowly like a woman in a dream, also came near, but paused before she reached him. At that moment, Roger Chillingworth pushed through the crowd and caught hold of the priest's arm.

'Stop!' he whispered to Mr Dimmesdale. 'What are you doing? Wave back that woman! Push away that child! All will be well. Do not do this! I can still save you!'

'You are too late!' answered the priest. 'With God's help, I shall escape you now!' He put out his hand to Hester.

'Hester Prynne! God has made me strong enough, at this last moment, to do the thing that I failed to do seven years ago. Come now, and be strong with me. Come and stand with me on the scaffold!'

There was great excitement in the crowd, but the priests

and magistrates could not believe what they were seeing, and they remained silent. They saw the young priest with Hester's arm around him, and his hand holding little Pearl's hand. The three of them climbed the steps of the scaffold, and were followed by old Roger Chillingworth.

'Is this the only place that you could find to escape from me?' whispered Chillingworth. 'The scaffold!'

'It is God who led me here!' said Mr Dimmesdale, 'and I thank Him for it.' But he trembled as he turned to Hester. 'Is this not better than what we planned in the forest?'

'I don't know!' she replied hurriedly. 'Better? We may both die, and little Pearl may die with us!'

'God will decide, but He is merciful,' said the priest. 'Let me do now what God has told me to do. I am a dying man, Hester. Let me accept my shame before I die.'

He turned and looked down at the crowd.

'People of New England!' he cried. 'You who have loved me! Look at me now, as I stand here with this woman. For seven long years you have called her a sinner and hated her. You have seen the scarlet letter on her bosom, and have crossed the street to avoid her. But there has been someone living among you whose sin and shame you have not known!' He stepped forward, away from Hester and the child. 'God knew him! The Devil knew him! And now, at the hour of his death, *you* shall know him! He stands in front of you! Look again at Hester's scarlet letter. With all its mysterious horror, it is only a shadow of what is on my own bosom! Look! Look! See for yourselves!'

And he pulled open his shirt for them to see his chest!

Cries of horror came from the crowd. For a moment, the priest stood proudly – a man who has won a battle over his own pain and fear. Then he fell to the ground.

Hester lifted him, and held his head against her bosom.

Hester lifted him, and held his head against her bosom.

Chillingworth knelt down beside him, an empty, dull look on his face.

'You have escaped me!' Chillingworth repeated again and again. 'You have escaped me!'

'May God forgive you,' the young priest said to him. 'You, too, have sinned deeply.' He turned his dying eyes towards Hester and the child. 'My little Pearl!' he said, his voice almost a whisper. 'Will you kiss me now?'

Pearl kissed him, and her tears fell on her father's face.

'Hester!' said the priest. 'Goodbye!'

'Won't we meet again?' she whispered, her face close to his. 'Won't we meet in heaven, and be together for ever?'

'Hester, Hester, I don't know,' he said. 'But God is merciful! He has proved his mercy. He gave me this burning pain to suffer on my bosom! He sent me that dark and terrible old man, to keep the pain always red-hot! He has brought me here, to die a death of shame, in front of the people! Without all this, I would be lost for ever! For this I thank Him. I thank God! Goodbye . . .!'

The final word came with the priest's dying breath.

10

Hester Prynne's sadness

After many days, when there had been time for people to arrange their thoughts, there was more than one report about what had been seen on the scaffold.

Most of those watching said that they saw a *scarlet letter*, like Hester Prynne's, on the priest's chest. But how long had it been there? There were various explanations, all of which were no more than guesses. Some said that Mr Dimmesdale had burned the letter into his chest on the same day that Hester Prynne received *her* scarlet letter. Others said that old Roger Chillingworth had caused it to appear, by some devilish magic. And others said it was a terrible sign of a guilty heart, and of God's punishment. The reader may choose from these possible explanations.

However, there were some who were watching who said that there was *no mark at all* on Mr Dimmesdale's chest. Neither, they said, had his dying words accepted any part of, or responsibility for, Hester Prynne's shame. The priest, they said, by choosing to die in the arms of that sinful woman, was simply trying to teach his people that even the most godly of them were all sinners in the eyes of God.

But nothing was more extraordinary than the way old

Roger Chillingworth changed after Mr Dimmesdale's death. This unhappy man grew weaker every day. Revenge had been his food and drink, and without it, his life had no meaning. Before the end of a year, he was dead.

But he left all his money – together with land and houses in England – to little Pearl, the daughter of Hester Prynne.

So Pearl became the richest person of those days in New England. This, of course, changed the way people behaved towards Hester and her daughter. Many families, thinking about the future, now saw Pearl, not as a child of sin, but as a most suitable wife for one of their sons! But soon after Chillingworth died, Hester and Pearl disappeared, and for many years no one knew where they had gone.

People told the story of the scarlet letter to their children, and their children's children. The scaffold where the poor priest died remained, and was as strong a warning of shame as it ever was.

And then, one afternoon, some children were playing near Hester's old cottage when they saw a tall woman in a grey dress go up to the door. In all those years it had never once been opened, but she seemed to unlock it before going inside. She turned in the doorway and looked back – long enough for those watching to see the scarlet letter on her bosom. Hester Prynne had returned!

But where was little Pearl, now a young woman? Was she alive or dead? No one knew, nor did they ever find out. But for the remainder of Hester's life, she received letters from England. And in the cottage were beautiful, expensive things

Hester Prynne had returned!

which Hester never used, but which spoke of somebody's loving thoughts towards her. And once, someone saw Hester decorating a baby's dress with the richest of gold thread.

All these things led people to believe that Pearl was not only alive but also married and happy. And that she did not forget

71

her mother and always kept her home in England open for her, if Hester should ever want it.

But Hester Prynne's life was in New England. Here she had sinned, and here she would end her life. She had returned willingly, and once again put on her scarlet letter.

Never again did it leave her bosom. However, in the years that followed, it became a sign not of shame but of sadness. It reminded others that here was a woman who had done wrong, but who had been punished enough. And people, especially women, came to her for advice, for her wise words, for comfort in their times of trouble and misery and suffering.

When she died, a new grave was dug next to an old one, but there was only one gravestone for the two graves. It was a simple stone – you may still see it there today – and on it was just one letter; a letter that had been scarlet, a letter that both began this sad story, and brought it to an end.

GLOSSARY

adultery sex between a married person and someone who is not their husband or wife

balcony a platform built on the upstairs outside wall of a building

bosom a woman's chest, or the part of her clothing that covers it

cheek either side of the face below the eyes

cottage a small, simple house, usually in the country

devil a bad, evil person (**the Devil** is the enemy of God)

election a time when people vote to choose a new government

evil very bad; harmful

forehead the part of the face above the eyes

forgive to stop feeling angry with someone who has done something to harm or annoy you

godly living a good life that follows the laws of your religion

Governor a person who controls part of a country

grave a hole in the ground where a dead person is buried

gravestone a stone on a grave showing the buried person's name

graveyard a piece of land near a church where people are buried

guilty having done something that is against the law

heaven the place where God is believed to live

Indians / Red Indians the original people in America before the white man came (*used in Hawthorne's time, but not acceptable today; people now use 'Native American' or 'American Indian'*)

innocent having done nothing wrong

joy a very happy feeling

magic making strange or mysterious things happen, which cannot easily be explained

magistrate a person who works as a judge in a court of law

Master *(old-fashioned)* a polite word for an important man

medical   of or about medicine or doctors

mercy   being kind and forgiving to somebody who has done wrong (*adj* **merciful**)

meteor   a piece of rock from outer space that burns brightly when it hits the Earth's air

Mistress *(old-fashioned)*   a polite word for a married woman

mood   the way you are feeling at a particular time

needle   a small thin piece of metal that you use for sewing

nervous   afraid, not confident

pale   with little colour in the face

partner   somebody you work with or have a relationship with

passion   a very strong feeling (of love, hate, anger, enthusiasm, etc.)

pray   to send a message, silent or spoken, to God

priest   an official at a church

public *(adj)*   able to be seen or known by everybody

Puritans   a group of Christians in the 16th and 17th centuries who believed in living a simple life with hard work and little fun

religion   a belief in a god or gods, and the different ways of showing the belief (*adj* **religious**)

respect *(v)*   to have a very good opinion of someone

scaffold   a high platform where criminals are killed in public

sermon   a talk on a religious subject, given by a priest

shame   feelings of guilt when you have done something wrong or sinful; or the loss of respect caused by wrongdoing or sin

sin   a very bad thing that your religion says you should not do

soul   the part of us that some people believe does not die

suffer   to feel pain or great sadness

thread   a long, thin piece of cotton, used with a needle for sewing

wise   sensible and experienced; showing good judgement

witch   a woman who uses magic to do evil things

wrong *(v)*   to behave badly or in an unfair way to someone

The Scarlet Letter

ACTIVITIES

Before Reading

1 **Read the story introduction on the first page of the book, and the back cover. Which of these ideas would *you* agree with, and which do you think the Puritans of New England would agree with?**

1 Adultery is a terrible sin which must be punished.

2 Adultery means a marriage has broken down and so it is best for everyone to finish the marriage.

3 It is more important to forgive than to punish.

4 You should be kind to somebody who has sinned, and help them to be good again.

5 You must never tell a lie.

6 If telling the truth will hurt another person, you should stay silent.

7 A child of adultery is a bad child, and must stay away from other children.

2 **Can you guess what happens to these people in the story? Choose as many answers as you like.**

Hester   Hester's child   Hester's lover   Hester's husband

1 . . . has a long life.

2 . . . has a short life.

3 . . . goes to prison.

4 . . . finds happiness.

5 . . . is punished for past sins.

6 . . . becomes a stronger person.

7 . . . leaves Boston.

8 . . . forgives a sinner.

ACTIVITIES

ACTIVITIES

While Reading

Read Chapters 1 and 2. Choose the best question-word for these questions and then answer them.

Who / What

1 . . . was in the old wooden box with the papers?
2 . . . punishments did the women suggest for Hester?
3 . . . could the magistrates send to the scaffold?
4 . . . was Hester's punishment for her sin?
5 . . . had probably died before reaching Massachusetts?
6 . . . name did Hester refuse to give to the priest?
7 . . . did the prison officer bring to see Hester?
8 . . . was Hester afraid that Roger would do to her and her child?
9 . . . did Roger want to find?
10 . . . did Roger want to do to this person?
11 . . . did Roger ask Hester to do?

Before you read Chapter 3, can you guess what difficulties Hester will face? For each sentence, circle Y (Yes) or N (No).

1 Someone tries to kill her. Y/N
2 The Puritans want to take her child away from her. Y/N
3 The women try to make her leave town. Y/N
4 People try to stop her getting any work. Y/N
5 Nobody in the shops will sell her any food. Y/N

**Read Chapters 3 to 5. Are these sentences true (T) or false (F)?
Rewrite the false ones with the correct information.**

1 People gave Hester a lot of work because they felt sorry for
her.
2 People wanted to take Pearl away from Hester and send her
to England.
3 Arthur thought that Pearl should stay with her mother.
4 As time passed, some people began to think that Roger
Chillingworth was sent by the Devil, not by God.
5 Arthur Dimmesdale often talked about the sickness of his
soul, but Chillingworth refused to listen.
6 When Arthur told people that he was a hateful sinner, they
believed him and talked about getting a new priest.
7 When Arthur saw Hester and Pearl, he asked them to go
away and leave him alone on the scaffold.
8 Arthur was able to stand on the scaffold at night, but he
was too afraid of public shame to do it in the daylight.

**Before you read Chapter 6, what advice would you give Hester
now? Choose some of these ideas.**

1 You should tell Roger that you will tell everyone his secret
unless he leaves Arthur alone.
2 You should tell Arthur to tell the world his secret.
3 You should tell Arthur to leave Boston.
4 You should leave Boston and make a new life somewhere
else.
5 You should tell Arthur the truth about Roger.

Read Chapters 6 to 8. Then match these halves of sentences.

1 Hester had the respect of many people now . . .

2 Roger had changed from a kind person into an evil one . . .

3 Hester wanted Roger to forgive her and Arthur and become a wise, kind man again . . .

4 Arthur thought life was easier for Hester . . .

5 Hester advised Arthur to leave Boston . . .

6 Arthur was worried about getting to know Pearl . . .

7 Pearl did not want to go to her mother . . .

8 Hester and Arthur decided to return to England . . .

9 . . . but Roger thought it was too late for that now.

10 . . . until she had put the scarlet letter back on her bosom.

11 . . . because everyone knew about her sin.

12 . . . because she worked hard and lived a godly life.

13 . . . because children did not usually like him.

14 . . . since there they could live a quiet life more easily.

15 . . . after he had spent seven years getting a cruel revenge.

16 . . . so that he could begin a happy life somewhere else.

Before you read the last chapters, try to guess what happens on Election Day. Choose some of these ideas, and then choose names to complete those sentences.

1 *Hester / Arthur / Pearl / Roger* will leave Boston on the ship.

2 *Roger / Arthur* will tell everyone who Pearl's father is.

3 *Hester / Arthur* will kill Roger.

4 *Hester / Arthur / Pearl* will stand on the scaffold together.

5 *Arthur / Roger* will die.

After Reading

1 **When Hester and Pearl sailed back to England, what did Hester tell Pearl about her life with Roger and Arthur? Complete their conversation (use as many words as you like).**

PEARL: Mother, why didn't your husband come with you to Boston?

HESTER: _____

PEARL: And how did you get to know my father?

HESTER : _____

PEARL: But how could you fall in love with him? You already had a husband, so it was a sin – breaking God's law.

HESTER : _____

PEARL: Two years! That's a long time. And when he suddenly appeared again, how did you feel?

HESTER : _____

PEARL: But why didn't he accuse my father in public?

HESTER : _____

PEARL: How horrible! Why didn't you tell me all this before, when my father was alive?

2 **Pearl's last question in the activity above is an interesting one. Here are some possible answers. Choose the one you think best and explain why you prefer it.**

1 You were too young to understand.

2 It was better for you not to know.

3 I didn't have the right to tell you other people's secrets.
4 Your father and my husband both had secrets, and children can't keep secrets.
5 If you didn't know, other people couldn't find things out from you.
6 I had wronged my husband, and I didn't want your father to go to prison, or die, so I had to keep their secrets from everybody. That meant you as well.

3 **Here are some quotes from the story. What do they tell us about the speakers, or other characters in the story?**

1 'Heaven has allowed you public shame, and the chance to win an open battle with the evil inside you and the sadness outside. Do you refuse to give him [the child's father] that same chance – which he may be too afraid to take himself?' *(Arthur, page 10)*

2 'It is not for some magistrate to take off this letter. When – if ever – I earn the right to be rid of it, it will fall off without anyone's help.' *(Hester, page 40)*

3 'You planted the evil, and now its black flowers are growing. We cannot change the way things are.' *(Roger, page 43)*

4 'That old man's revenge has been blacker than our sin, Hester!' *(Arthur, page 49)*

5 'What a strange, sad man he is. He held your hand and mine at night on the scaffold, and again in the forest. But here on this sunny day, among all the people, he does not know us, and we must not speak to him.' *(Pearl, page 60)*

4 Look at these words from the story. Which heading would you put them under? Can some words go under more than one heading? Is there any word which does not belong under any heading?

FEELINGS	THE LAW	RELIGION	SEWING
cloth	magistrate	pattern	revenge
godly	material	priest	sermon
guilty	mercy	prison	shame
heaven	misery	punishment	sin
innocent	needle	Puritan	soul
joy	passion	respect	thread

5 This is how one of the townspeople described Arthur Dimmesdale's last moments. Put the parts of sentences in the right order, and join them with the best linking word from each pair. Begin with number 4.

1 He stood there in front of the crowd and cried out

2 *after / but* he pushed the doctor away

3 *if / because* almost at once the priest fell to the ground.

4 Yes, I was there, quite close to Mr Dimmesdale

5 *yet / and* climbed up onto the scaffold with Mistress Prynne and the child.

6 *However, / Whatever,* the poor child did not have a father for very long,

7 *that / to* see the great, scarlet letter 'A' on his chest,

8 *While / After* little Pearl had kissed him,

9 *though / when* he stopped next to the scaffold

10 *whether / that* he was as great a sinner as Hester Prynne.

11 *and then / now that* he died in Mistress Prynne's arms.

12 *and / or* called out to Mistress Prynne and her little girl.

13 *Meanwhile, / Finally,* he pulled open his shirt for us

14 The old doctor hurried up to him and caught his arm,

15 he thanked God for his mercy,

16 *who / which* means, of course, that he is the father of Hester Prynne's child!

6 Imagine that you could give the story a different ending. Choose one of the endings below, and use the notes to write a paragraph. Which ending – including the original one – do you prefer, and why?

• Arthur confesses on scaffold / does not die / sails to England with Hester and Pearl (What happens to Roger?)

• Arthur does not confess / leaves with Hester and Pearl for new life somewhere in America (Does Roger stay or go?)

• Arthur does not confess / Roger tells Arthur's secret / Arthur goes to prison / Hester and Pearl go on living in Boston

• Arthur confesses / goes to prison / Hester sent back to Roger / dies mysteriously (What happens to Pearl?)

7 If you could choose a different letter for Hester to wear, which word would it be for – S for sinful, B for brave? Choose a letter for Hester, Roger, Arthur, and Pearl to wear, and explain why that word says something important about that character.

ABOUT THE AUTHOR

Nathaniel Hawthorne was born in Salem, Massachusetts, in 1804, into a family which had come to America with the first Puritan settlers. While still a boy, Hawthorne wrote to his mother that 'I do not want to be a doctor and live by men's diseases; nor a minister to live by their sins; nor a lawyer and live by their quarrels. So I don't see there is anything left for me but to be an author.' After college, Hawthorne returned to Salem and wrote stories, including some for children, and a novel, but he did not achieve success quickly.

For a time he worked in the Boston custom house, and later in the port of Salem. In 1850 he had his first big success with *The Scarlet Letter*, drawing on his knowledge of New England and Puritan life. *The House of the Seven Gables* (1851) also dealt with problems of guilt and sin. From 1853 to 1857 Hawthorne was American consul at Liverpool in England, and then spent two years in Italy, the setting for his novel *The Marble Faun* (1860). He then returned to America, where he died in 1864.

Hawthorne is considered one of the great American writers. Questions of sin, crime, suffering, and guilt are never far away in his work, and his view of life is a dark one. *The Scarlet Letter* is still one of the most respected works of American literature. It has been made into a play and a musical, and filmed eleven times, though one film, made in the 1990s and starring Demi Moore, annoyed many Americans. This film version had an attack by Indians, naked swimming, and Arthur and Hester riding away together in a happy ending, which of course changes Hawthorne's story completely.

OXFORD BOOKWORMS LIBRARY

Classics • Crime & Mystery • Factfiles • Fantasy & Horror
Human Interest • Playscripts • Thriller & Adventure
True Stories • World Stories

The OXFORD BOOKWORMS LIBRARY provides enjoyable reading in English, with a wide range of classic and modern fiction, non-fiction, and plays. It includes original and adapted texts in seven carefully graded language stages, which take learners from beginner to advanced level. An overview is given on the next pages.

All Stage 1 titles are available as audio recordings, as well as over eighty other titles from Starter to Stage 6. All Starters and many titles at Stages 1 to 4 are specially recommended for younger learners. Every Bookworm is illustrated, and Starters and Factfiles have full-colour illustrations.

The OXFORD BOOKWORMS LIBRARY also offers extensive support. Each book contains an introduction to the story, notes about the author, a glossary, and activities. Additional resources include tests and worksheets, and answers for these and for the activities in the books. There is advice on running a class library, using audio recordings, and the many ways of using Oxford Bookworms in reading programmes. Resource materials are available on the website <www.oup.com/bookworms>.

The *Oxford Bookworms Collection* is a series for advanced learners. It consists of volumes of short stories by well-known authors, both classic and modern. Texts are not abridged or adapted in any way, but carefully selected to be accessible to the advanced student.

———————

You can find details and a full list of titles in the *Oxford Bookworms Library Catalogue* and *Oxford English Language Teaching Catalogues*, and on the website <www.oup.com/bookworms>.

THE OXFORD BOOKWORMS LIBRARY
GRADING AND SAMPLE EXTRACTS

STARTER • 250 HEADWORDS

present simple – present continuous – imperative –
can/cannot, must – *going to* (future) – simple gerunds ...

Her phone is ringing – but where is it?

Sally gets out of bed and looks in her bag. No phone. She looks under the bed. No phone. Then she looks behind the door. There is her phone. Sally picks up her phone and answers it. *Sally's Phone*

STAGE 1 • 400 HEADWORDS

... past simple – coordination with *and, but, or* –
subordination with *before, after, when, because, so* ...

I knew him in Persia. He was a famous builder and I worked with him there. For a time I was his friend, but not for long. When he came to Paris, I came after him – I wanted to watch him. He was a very clever, very dangerous man. *The Phantom of the Opera*

STAGE 2 • 700 HEADWORDS

... present perfect – *will* (future) – *(don't) have to, must not, could* –
comparison of adjectives – simple *if* clauses – past continuous –
tag questions – *ask/tell* + infinitive ...

While I was writing these words in my diary, I decided what to do. I must try to escape. I shall try to get down the wall outside. The window is high above the ground, but I have to try. I shall take some of the gold with me – if I escape, perhaps it will be helpful later. *Dracula*

... should, may – present perfect continuous – *used to* – past perfect –
causative – relative clauses – indirect statements ...

Of course, it was most important that no one should see
Colin, Mary, or Dickon entering the secret garden. So Colin
gave orders to the gardeners that they must all keep away
from that part of the garden in future. ***The Secret Garden***

STAGE 4 • 1400 HEADWORDS

... past perfect continuous – passive (simple forms) –
would conditional clauses – indirect questions –
relatives with *where/when* – gerunds after prepositions/phrases ...

I was glad. Now Hyde could not show his face to the world
again. If he did, every honest man in London would be proud
to report him to the police. ***Dr Jekyll and Mr Hyde***

STAGE 5 • 1800 HEADWORDS

... future continuous – future perfect –
passive (modals, continuous forms) –
would have conditional clauses – modals + perfect infinitive ...

If he had spoken Estella's name, I would have hit him. I was so
angry with him, and so depressed about my future, that I could
not eat the breakfast. Instead I went straight to the old house.
Great Expectations

STAGE 6 • 2500 HEADWORDS

... passive (infinitives, gerunds) – advanced modal meanings –
clauses of concession, condition

When I stepped up to the piano, I was confident. It was as if I
knew that the prodigy side of me really did exist. And when I
started to play, I was so caught up in how lovely I looked that
I didn't worry how I would sound. ***The Joy Luck Club***

Persuasion

JANE AUSTEN

Retold by Clare West

At nineteen Anne Elliot refuses an offer of marriage from Frederick Wentworth, persuaded to do so by Lady Russell, a friend of her dead mother. Wentworth is a sailor, with no money and an uncertain future, says Lady Russell – just a nobody, certainly not worthy of a baronet's daughter.

Eight years later Wentworth returns, a rich and successful captain, looking for a wife. Anne is still unmarried, but Captain Wentworth clearly prefers the company of the two Musgrove girls . . .

Jane Austen's tale of love and marriage is told with humour and a sharp understanding of human behaviour.

A Morbid Taste for Bones

ELLIS PETERS

Retold by John Escott

Murder in the twelfth century is no different from murder today. There is still a dead body, though this time with an arrow through the heart instead of a bullet. There is still a need to bury the dead, to comfort the living – and to catch the murderer.

When Brother Cadfael comes to a village in the Welsh hills, he finds himself doing all three of those things. And there is nothing simple about this death. The murdered man's daughter needs Cadfael's help in more ways than one. There are questions about the arrow. And the burial is the strangest thing of all . . .